CW00665712

www.JewishPoem.com
Instagram.com/JewishPoems

still here: jewish
poems about oct 7 &
beyond

lior avraham

dedicated to every
jewish person and
those who fight for
us

but he was pierced for
our transgressions,
crushed for our
iniquities.
the chastisement for our
peace was upon him,
and by his stripes we are
healed.

isaiah 53:5

how many times
will you try to erase us
before you accept that
we're
not
going
anywhere

Each time I lose a friend
it hurts
but not as much as it does
imagining a toddler
in a tunnel
so go
goodbye
my people need me
more than I need you

lior avraham

have you seen
a red-headed boy?
small
with a little brother
and mother
and father
and about 200
aunts and uncles?
have you seen
a red-headed boy?

I have not moved on
frozen in time
every day is
oct 8
waking up
can it be true?
was it a dream?
we're not a people
who let go
who move on
until everyone is
home

lior avraham

we survived
pogroms
expulsions
camps
what do you think
a fruit emoji
can do

how can
it never happened
and
resistance is justified
both be true

lior avraham

it never made me happy
to see buildings on fire
or babies
lost
families wailing
i didn't cheer
the way you did
when it was us

shiri
mother of flame haired dragons
you family has united a nation

hersh
you are known by your mother's unfailing
fight
she is now the fiercest of
warriors

yarden
we have seen your wedding video
the tenderness of your eyes reflects
our love for you
and each
and every
soul
we are
waiting for

lior avraham

me too
unless she's a jew

indigenous rights
unless some are too light

defend your people
in a way that's not lethal
even when men hide
behind babies
blur innocence and evil
so when both are gone
the world screams

then the world
finally screams

if they only
love you
if you are willing
to separate yourself
from your
homeland

they don't love you
they love
watching
you
wander

lior avraham

we're not anti-you
just
anti-you-having-a-place-to-go
when we become
anti-you
again

i imagine telling
abraham, moshe, king david
that they've managed to
convince some of us
that we're not from the
land that bears our name

they would ask:
where do they say we're from
"nowhere."

why are they saying this?
"they're afraid."

lior avraham

if you have to
join with those
who say you are from
nowhere
to feel safe

you may need
the homeland
more than you
realize

they don't
believe us
even with
video
audio
live streamed
from the
chests of proud
killers

but how
quickly
do absurdities
become facts
when we
are the
villains

lior avraham

at one point
you realize
they have no
intention
of understanding

they take delight
in watching us
explain
defend

save your breath
for dandelions
and prayers

they
know

they
know

but there is
something in
the air
that thirsts for
jewish tears

they know

lior avraham

it's ok
to rest

lay down
in green
pastures

close your
eyes
beside
still waters

as Hashem
restores
your
soul

naama
bibas
all

we are
fighting
for you

when it
gets hard

we see
your
eyes

hold on

lior avraham

if we are the
colonizers

why are all
of our ancient
clay and bronze
treasures
buried here

why are the bones
of our ancestors
and kings
buried here

why does this place bear
our name
why is your temple
built atop ours

if we are the colonizers
why is this land
and our people
mentioned
in your holy book

why are our prophets
your prophets

why does our
faith
predate yours

you build on top of us
and then
call
us the
invaders

lior avraham

"colonizer!"

he yelled
from his ranch-style
apartment built atop
former miwok
land

"invader"

she screamed
while
sipping a latte
in gentrified
brooklyn

i have seen
gazans
with green
eyes

light skin

pale hair

are they
any less
palestinian?

lior avraham

it's not my wish
to shame the silent
among us

but how
do you watch
your
kinsman
fight
bleed
rally

and do
nothing

the silence of strangers
i understand

they have no skin in this war

but how do you
whose grandmother
whispered stories of
survival
at your time of battle
choose to protect your
aesthetic
over your
people

lior avraham

esther was
scared
too

but maybe

maybe

you were
born
for
such
a
time
as
this

it's either
stand up
now

or
line up
later

lior avraham

if you
have to
stay silent
to
stay safe

you're already
in
great
danger

22 arab
countries

one jewish
nation

that existed
before
islam
took its
first breath

but somehow
we are
the
colonizers

lior avraham

they
don't
love
you

they
love
watching
you
hate
yourself

22 arab
nations

one jewish
state

that existed
before
islam
took its
first breath

but somehow
we are
the
colonizers

lior avraham

we will
not
apologize
for
existing

they enjoy
watching you
explain
defend
explain

because some
demons
feast
only
on
earnestness

lior avraham

they
want they
keep you
explaining

to keep
you
from
living

another day

another
accusation

lior avraham

it's not
hatred

it's envy

joseph's brothers
didn't hate him

until the jacket
and the dream

sometimes I ask
hashem
why
being chosen
means being
hated

light bearers
repel darkness
we carry the torah
in a word
that wants
no rules

lior avraham

if we
control
the
media

why
are we
hated
by
it

the hatred
of jews
is rooted
in
envy

lior avraham

all
you've
done
is
made
us
stronger

if
hatred
could
kill
us
we'd
already
be gone

lior avraham

everything
changes
when you
realize

they are
more
committed
to
their
stories

than the
truth

"stop acting
like the
victim"

they said
to the
one year old
in the
tunnel

lior avraham

it's amazing
how
when it
comes
to
jewsish
people

lies are so
easily
devoured

the un
quietly
halved the
number of
dead

the un
quietly
admitted
women
were telling
the truth

they
quietly
admitted
there's no famine

why are the lies
so loud
and the truth
barely above a
whisper

lior avraham

"free palestine"

we're trying

jewish people
have
never
colonized

but
ask
algeria
tunisia
iran
and the like
who turned
their world
upside
down

lior avraham

free palestine
from
westerners
desperate
to
feel
important

free palestine
from
those who
hate jews
more than they
value
innocent
blood

if
hezbollah
isis
and
iran's leader
all
agree
with you

you might
be wrong

lior avraham

i miss the
good old days

when grapes
were cheap

and everyone
knew
isis
was bad

jewish people
don't kill
while screaming
"baruch Hashem!"

we don't fly
planes into
buildings

we don't
blow ourselves up
conquer lands
spread our faith
or language

we grow gardens
toast to life
light candles to remember
and eat

lior avraham

any doubt
that israel
is blessed
is gone

only a place
blessed
from
above would
receive so
much
hate
from
below

free
palestine

from students
desperate
for
virtue

lior avraham

free
palestine

from
billionaires
who call
the shots
from
qatari
mansions

free palestine

from the
belief

that
freedom

can be
purchased

in blood

lior avraham

the person
who
justifies
those who
kill us

hates us
as just
as much
as the one
who
holds
the knife

there
are
people
in
the
tunnels
who
believed
in
peace

lior avraham

"they're not
all bad."

of course not.

but ask
your friend
if they
can call
a killer
a killer
before inviting
them
inside

Hashem
protect
your
people
from a
chronic
desire
to earn
the approval
of those
who
hate
us

lior avraham

before you
take
the
high
road
make sure
it's
not
just a
bad
place
to hide

the
calendar
lies

today
is oct 7

maybe
oct 8

but never
a
day
past
that

lior avraham

save us
Hashem
from
thinking
the ones
who
choose
the fence
when our backs
are against
the wall
are our
friends

they took
our prophets
borrowed from
our holy books
built a
temple atop
ours
refuse us entry
into their lands
while we host
in ours
despite the cost

and yet
they want more
they want it all
but we are the
invaders

lior avraham

"____phobic"

it's not
a phobia
if
they
want
to kill
you

because
some
aren't brave
enough to
do it
changes nothing

never forget
that even
live video
from the chests
of
monsters

wasn't
enough
proof

lior avraham

save your
breath
for
i love yous

because
there are
people
who would rather
believe
a lie
than
a jew

we aren't
the
evil

we're holding
it back

because we know
if it
conquers us
it will
come for
you
next

lior avraham

"as a jew…"

darling

they'll
never pick you

when they're
done with us

when they no longer
need you as a blanket
concealing
their hatred

you will be
next

to be both called
a white
supremacist
and
hated
by
white supremacists
is a
strange thing
indeed

lior avraham

they pretend
we don't
come in
all shades
from
freshly milled flour
to
fragrant vanilla
bean
sweet brown sugars
creamy milk &
rich egg yolks

risen not with yeast
but with the breath
of Hashem

we are
the ingredients
for the sweetest
of breads

the
difference
between us
and them
is that
we watch
gazans
beaten
bloody by
hamas
for taking
food rightly
theirs
and
hate it

lior avraham

how can we
be white
supremacists
and hated by
white
supremacists

they
refused
to let
us mourn

so we
stopped
asking
for
permission

lior avraham

the
difference
between us
and them is
that we
watch gazans
beaten
bloody by
hamas for
taking food
rightly
theirs and
hate it

lior avraham

the difference
between us
and them

is that
we watch
gazans
beaten bloody
by hamas
for taking food
rightly theirs

and
hate it

lior avraham

there are
so many
reasons
to be
depressed

but even
in the
dark hours

remember

we are
a people

chosen

to bring
light

lior avraham

every
100 years
the ancient
hatred

changes into
fresh
clothes

thinking
we won't
recognize
its
scent

lior avraham

wanted:

all of
the
hostages

home
safe
tears wiped
wounds tended
hot meal eaten

we will
tuck them into
a soft, clean bed
kiss their
foreheads
and whisper

never
again

lior avraham

if we can
feel
the sun's
warmth
from
152 million
kilometers away

naama, shiri, kfir
and
everyone

can certainly
feel the
ferocity of
our love

we are a
million
scattered
suns

lior avraham

we are
the
nation
Hashem chose
to carry
light

to carry
a zeal
and respect
for
life

they don't
hate us
they hate
what
we
stand for

lior avraham

there
have always
been lies

a spoonful
of
slander
helps the
antisemitism
go
down

lior avraham

we're
still
here

despite
all the ways
you've tried
to end us

we're
still
here

lior avraham

they know
they're wrong

people fighting
for good
don't
dress like
bandits

lior avraham

they love
watching us
fall
over our words
scramble to
explain
defend
fight

because they know
what we have inside
is timeless
indestructible
Hashem given
so they
settle
for
a bit
of
sweat

lior avraham

i get
tired

want to
put down
my
sword

then i
remember kfir

and wonder

when's the
last time
he saw
the
sun

lior avraham

as summer
fades
into
autumn

the
masses
loses
interest

but we're
still
here

lior avraham

naama
daniela
agam
karina
liri

forgive us

we're trying

lior avraham

naama
daniela
agam
karina
liri

you should
be making
silly videos

daydreaming
into journals

laying on
beaches

singing with
siblings

we hate
this

lior avraham

avera
mengistu

we have
not
forgotten

our brother

lior avraham

naama
daniela
agam
karina
liri

you
are a
nation's
daughters

a nation's
sisters

we
are
coming

lior avraham

we
 think

of you

every
day

every hour

every minute

lior avraham

hear
o
israel

lior avraham

they day
they
brought
noa
and our boys

my soul burst
heart leapt

joy
unspeakable

again

lior avraham

to all
who have lost
someone

you don't
weep
alone

lior avraham

i am not
pregnant

but i
eat for two
dance for two
lay
on the grass
in the sun
for
two

everything
i
do
i do
for me
and a brother
or
sister
taken

lior avraham

still here: jewish poems about oct 7 and beyond

thank you
to
our
men and
women

in olive
green

gideons
and deborahs

davids
and
yaels

lior avraham

they
will
come
home

lior avraham

they didn't
create us

they
can't
end
us

lior avraham

to ever

single

jewish
soul

i love you

still here: jewish poems about oct 7 and beyond

never

ever

again

lior avraham

this too
we
survived

lior avraham

Printed in Great Britain
by Amazon